A SHORT METHOD
OF PRAYER

A SHORT METHOD
OF PRAYER

J.M.B. DE LA MOTHE GUYON

Translated from the Paris Edition of 1790

A NEW PRAYER PRESS BOOK

BOOK INFORMATION

A New Prayer Press Book
Published by Wildside Press, LLC
www.wildsidebooks.com

AUTHOR'S PREFACE

I did not write this little work with the thought of its being given to the public. It was prepared for the help of a few Christians who were desirous of loving God with the whole heart. But so many have requested copies of it, because of the benefit they have derived from its perusal, that I have been asked to publish it.

I have left it in its natural simplicity. I do not condemn the opinions of any: on the contrary, I esteem those which are held by others, and submit all that I have written to the censure of persons of experience and learning. I only ask of all that they will not be content with examining the outside, but that they will penetrate the design of the writer, which is only to lead others to *love* God, and to serve Him with greater happiness and success, by enabling them to do it in a simple and easy way, fit for the little ones who are not capable of extraordinary things, but who truly desire to *give themselves to God.*

I ask all who may read it, to read without prejudice; and they will discover, under common expressions, a hidden unction, which will lead them to seek for a happiness which all ought to expect to possess.

I use the word *facility*, saying that perfection is easy, because it is easy to find God, *when we seek Him within ourselves.* The passage may be quoted which says, "Ye shall seek me, and shall not find me" (John vii. 34). Yet this need not occasion any difficulty; because the same God, who cannot contradict Himself, has said, "He that seeketh findeth" (Matt. vii. 8). *He who seeks*

God, and who yet is unwilling to forsake sin, will not find Him, because he is seeking Him where He cannot be found; therefore it is added, "Ye shall die in your sins." *But he who sincerely desires to forsake sin, that he may draw near to God, will find Him infallibly.*

Many people imagine religion so frightful, and prayer so extraordinary, that they are not willing to strive after them, never expecting to attain to them. But as the difficulty which we see in a thing causes us to despair of succeeding in it, and at the same time removes the desire to undertake it; and as, when a thing appears both desirable and easy to be attained, we give ourselves to it with pleasure, and pursue it boldly; I have been constrained to set forth the advantage and the *facility* of this way.

Oh! if we were persuaded of the goodness of God toward His poor creatures, and of the desire which He has to communicate Himself to them, we should not imagine so many obstacles, and despair so easily of obtaining a good which He is so infinitely desirous of imparting to us.

And if He has not spared His own Son, but delivered Him up for us all, is there anything He can refuse us? Assuredly not. We only need a little courage and perseverance. We have so much of both for trifling temporal interests, and we have none for the *"one thing needful."*

As for those who find a difficulty in believing that it is easy to find God in this way, let them not believe all that they are told, but rather let them make trial of it, that they may judge for themselves; and they will find that I say very little in comparison with that which is.

Dear reader, study this little work with a simple and sincere heart, with lowliness of mind, without wishing to criticise it, and you will find it of good to you. Receive it with the same spirit as that in which it is given, which is no other than the longing that you may be led to *give yourself unreservedly to God.* My desire is that it may be the means of leading the simple ones and the children to their Father, who loves their humble confidence, and to whom distrust is so displeasing. Seek nothing but *the love of God*; have a sincere desire for your salvation, and you will assuredly find it, following this little unmethodical method.

I do not pretend to elevate my sentiments above those of others, but I relate simply what has been my own experience as well as that of others, and the advantage which I have found in this simple and natural manner of going to God.

If this book treats of nothing else but the *short and easy method of prayer*, it is because, being written only for that, it cannot speak of other things. It is certain that, if it be read in the spirit in which it has been written, there will be found nothing in it to shock the mind. Those who will make the experience of it will be the most certain of the truth which it contains.

It is to Thee, O Holy Child Jesus, who lovest simplicity and innocence, and who findest Thy delight in the children of men, that is to say, with those amongst men who are willing to become children;—it is to Thee, I say, to give worth and value to this little work, impressing it on the heart, and leading those who read it to seek Thee within themselves, where Thou wilt take Thy rest, receiving the tokens of their love, and giving them proofs of Thine.

It is Thy work, O Divine Child! O uncreated Love! O silent Word! to make Thyself beloved, tasted, and heard. Thou art able to do it; and I even dare to say that Thou wilt do it, by means of this little work, which is all to Thee, all of Thee, and all for Thee.

CHAPTER I

ALL ARE COMMANDED TO PRAY—PRAYER THE GREAT MEANS OF SALVATION, AND POSSIBLE AT ALL TIMES BY THE MOST SIMPLE.

Prayer is nothing else but the *application of the heart to God,* and the interior exercise of love. St Paul commands us to "pray without ceasing" (1 Thess. v. 17). Our Lord says: "Take ye heed, watch and pray." "And what I say unto you, I say unto all" (Mark xiii. 33, 37). All, then, are capable of prayer, and it is the duty of all to engage in it.

But I do not think that all are fit for meditation; and, therefore, it is not that sort of prayer which God demands or desires of them.

My dear friends, whoever you may be, who desire to be saved, come unto God in prayer. "I counsel thee to buy of me gold tried in the fire, that thou mayest be rich" (Rev. iii. 18). It is easily to be obtained, far more easily than you could ever imagine.

Come, all ye that are athirst, and take this water of life freely (see Rev. xxii. 17). Do not amuse yourselves by hewing out to yourselves "broken cisterns that can hold no water" (Jer. ii. 13). Come, hungry souls, who find nothing that can satisfy you, and you shall be *filled.* Come, poor afflicted ones, weighed down with griefs and sorrows, and you shall be comforted. Come, sick ones, to the great Physician, and do not fear to approach Him because you are so weak and diseased: expose all your diseases to Him, and they shall be healed.

Come, children, to your Father; He will receive you with open arms of love. Come, wandering and scattered sheep, to your Shepherd. Come, sinners, to your Saviour. Come, ignorant and foolish ones, who believe yourselves incapable of prayer; it is you who are the most fitted for it. Come all without exception; Jesus Christ calls you all.

Let those only refuse to come who have no heart. The invitation is not for them; for we must have a heart in order to love. But who is indeed without heart? Oh, come and give that heart to God, and learn in the place of prayer how to do it! All those who long for prayer are capable of it, who have ordinary grace and the gift of the Holy Spirit, which is freely promised to all who ask it.

Prayer is the key of perfection and of sovereign happiness; it is the efficacious means of getting rid of all vices and of acquiring all virtues; for the way to become perfect is to live in the presence of God. He tells us this Himself: "Walk before me, and be thou perfect" (Gen. xvii. 1). Prayer alone can bring you into His presence, and keep you there continually.

What we need, then, is an attitude of prayer, in which we can *constantly* abide, and out of which exterior occupations cannot draw us; a prayer which can be offered alike by princes, kings, prelates, magistrates, soldiers, children, artisans, labourers, women, and the sick. This prayer is not mental, but *of the heart*.

It is not a prayer of thought alone, because the mind of man is so limited, that while it is occupied with one thing it cannot be thinking of another. But it is the PRAYER OF THE HEART, which cannot be interrupted by the occupations of the mind. Nothing can interrupt the prayer of the heart but unruly affections; and when once we have tasted of the love of God, it is impossible to find our delight in anything but Himself.

Nothing is easier than to have God and to live upon Him. He is more truly in us than we are in ourselves. He is more anxious to give Himself to us than we are to possess Him. All that we want is to know the way to seek Him, which is so easy and so natural, that breathing itself is not more so.

Oh, you who imagine yourselves incapable of religious feeling, you may live in prayer and in God as easily and as continuously as you live by the air you breathe. Will you not, then, be inexcusable if you neglect to do it, after you have learned the way?

CHAPTER II

FIRST DEGREE OF PRAYER—MEDITATION
AND MEDITATIVE READING—THE
LORD'S PRAYER—PASSAGE FROM THE
FIRST DEGREE TO THE SECOND.

There are two means by which we may be led into the higher forms of prayer. One is *Meditation*, the other is *Meditative Reading*. By meditative reading I mean the taking of some truths, either doctrinal or practical—the latter rather than the former—and reading them in this way:—Take the truth which has presented itself to you, and read two or three lines, seeking to enter into the full meaning of the words, and go on no further so long as you find satisfaction in them; leave the place only when it becomes insipid. After that, take another passage, and do the same, not reading more than half a page at once.

It is not so much from the amount read that we derive profit, as from the manner of reading. Those people who get through so much do not profit from it; the bees can only draw the juice from the flowers by resting on them, not by flying round them. Much reading is more for scholastic than for spiritual science; but in order to derive profit from spiritual books, we should read them in this way; and I am sure that this manner of reading accustoms us gradually to prayer, and gives us a deeper desire for it. The other way is *Meditation*, in which we should engage at a chosen time, and not in the hour given to reading. I think the way to enter into it is this:—After having brought ourselves into the presence of God by a definite act of faith, we should read something substantial, not so much to reason upon it, as to fix the attention, observing that the principal exercise should be the presence of God, and that the subject should rather fix the attention than exercise reason.

This *faith in the presence of God within our hearts* must lead us to enter within ourselves, collecting our thoughts, and preventing their wandering; this is an effectual way of getting rid of distracting thoughts, and of losing sight of outward things, in order to draw near to God, who can only be found in the secret place of our hearts, which is the *sancta-sanctorum* in which He dwells.

He has promised that if any one keeps His commandments, He will come to him, and *make His abode* with him (John xiv. 23). St Augustine reproaches himself for the time he lost through not having sought God at first in this way.

When, then, we are thus buried in ourselves, and deeply penetrated with the presence of God within us—when the senses are all drawn from the circumference to the centre, which, though it is not easily accomplished at first, becomes quite natural afterwards—when the soul is thus gathered up within itself, and is sweetly occupied with the truth read, not in reasoning upon it, but in feeding upon it, and exciting the will by the affection rather than the understanding by consideration: the *affection* being thus touched, must be suffered to *repose* sweetly and at peace, *swallowing* what it has tasted.

As a person who only masticated an excellent meat would not be nourished by it, although he would be sensible of its taste, unless he ceased this movement in order to swallow it; so when the affection is stirred, if we seek continually to stir it, we extinguish its fire, and thus deprive the soul of its nourishment. We must swallow by a *loving repose* (full of respect and confidence) what we have masticated and tasted. This method is very necessary, and would advance the soul in a short time more than any other would do in several years.

But as I said that the direct and principal exercise should be the *sense of the presence of God*, we must most faithfully *recall the senses* when they wander.

This is a short and efficacious way of fighting with distractions; because those who endeavour directly to oppose them, irritate and increase them; but by losing ourselves in the thought of a present God, and suffering our thoughts to be drawn to Him, we combat them indirectly, and without thinking of them, but in an effectual manner. And here let me warn beginners not to run from one truth to another, from one subject to another; but to keep themselves to one so long as they feel a taste for it: this is the way to enter deeply into truths, to taste them, and to have them impressed upon us. I say it is difficult at first thus to retire within ourselves, because of the habits, which are natural to us, of being taken up with the outside; but when we are a little accustomed to it, it becomes exceedingly easy; both because we have formed the habit of it, and because God, who only desires to communicate Himself to us, sends us abundant grace, and an experimental sense of His presence, which renders it easy.

Let us apply this method to the Lord's Prayer. We say "Our Father," thinking that God is within us, and will indeed be our Father. After having pronounced this word *Father*, we remain a few moments in silence, waiting for this heavenly Father to make known His will to us. Then we ask this King of Glory *to reign* within us, abandoning ourselves to Him, that He may do it, and yielding to Him the right that He has over us. If we feel here an inclination to peace and silence, we should not continue, but remain thus so long as the condition may last; after which we proceed to the second petition, "Thy will be done on earth, as it is in heaven." We then desire that God may accomplish, in us and by us, all His will; we give up to God our heart and our liberty, that He may dispose of them at His pleasure. Then, seeing that the occupation of the will should be love, we desire to love, and we ask God to give us *His love*. But all this is done quietly, peacefully; and so on with the rest of the prayer.

At other times we hold ourselves in the position of sheep near to the Shepherd, asking of Him our true food. O Divine Shepherd! Thou feedest Thy sheep with Thine own hand, and Thou art their food from day to day. We may also bring before Him our family desires; but it must all be done with the remembrance by faith of the presence of God within us.

We can form no imagination of what God is: a lively faith in His presence is sufficient; for we can conceive no image of God, though we may of Christ, regarding Him as crucified, or as a child, or in some other condition, provided that we always seek Him within ourselves.

At other times we come to Him as to a Physician, bringing our maladies to Him that He may heal them; but always without effort, with a short silence from time to time, that the silence may be mingled with the action, gradually lengthening the silence and shortening the spoken prayer, until at length, as we yield to the operation of God, He gains the supremacy. When the presence of God is given, and the soul begins to taste of silence and repose, this experimental sense of the presence of God introduces it to the second degree of prayer.

CHAPTER III

SECOND DEGREE OF PRAYER, CALLED HERE "THE PRAYER OF SIMPLICITY."

The second degree has been variously termed *Contemplation*, *The Prayer of Silence*, and *of repose*; while others again have called it the *Prayer of Simplicity*; and it is of this last term that I shall make use here, being more appropriate than that of *Contemplation*, which signifies a degree of prayer more advanced than that of which I speak.

After a time, as I have said, the soul becomes sensible of a facility in recognising the presence of God; it collects itself more easily; prayer becomes natural and pleasant; it knows that it leads to God; and it perceives the smell of His perfumes.

Then it must change its method, and observe carefully what I am about to say, without being astonished at its apparent implausibility.

First of all, when you bring yourself into the presence of God by faith, remain a short time in an attitude of respectful silence. If from the beginning, in making this act of faith, you are sensible of a little taste of the presence of God, remain as you are without troubling yourself on any subject, and keep that which has been given you, so long as it may remain.

If it leaves you, excite your will by means of some tender affection, and if you then find that your former state of peace has returned, remain in it. The fire must be blown softly, and as soon as it is lighted, cease to blow it, or you will put it out. It is also necessary that you should go to God, not so much to obtain something from Him, as to please Him, and to do His will; for a servant who only serves his master in proportion to the recompense he receives, is unworthy of any remuneration.

Go, then, to prayer, not only to enjoy God, but to be as He wills: this will keep you equal in times of barrenness and in times of abundance; and you will not be dismayed by the repulses of God, nor by His apparent indifference.

CHAPTER IV

ON SPIRITUAL DRYNESS.

As God's only desire is to give Himself to the loving soul who desires to seek Him, He often hides Himself in order to arouse it, and compel it to seek Him with love and fidelity. But how does He reward the faithfulness of His beloved! And how are His apparent flights followed by loving caresses!

The soul imagines that it is a proof of its fidelity and of its increased love that it seeks God with an effort, or that at least such seeking will soon lead to His return.

But no! This is not the way in this degree. With a loving impatience, with deep humility and abasement, with an affection deep and yet restful, with a respectful silence, you must await the return of your Beloved.

You will thus show Him that it is *Himself* alone that you love, and His good pleasure, and not the pleasure that you find in loving Him. Therefore it is said, "Make not haste in time of trouble. Cleave unto Him, and depart not away, that thou mayest be increased at thy last end" (Ecclus. ii. 2, 3). Suffer the suspensions and the delays of the visible consolations of God.

Be patient in prayer, even though you should do nothing all your life but wait in patience, with a heart humbled, abandoned, resigned, and content for the return of your Beloved. Oh, excellent prayer! How it moves the heart of God, and obliges Him to return more than anything else!

CHAPTER V

ABANDONMENT TO GOD—ITS FRUIT
AND ITS IRREVOCABILITY—IN WHAT IT
CONSISTS—GOD EXHORTS US TO IT.

It is here that true *abandonment* and consecration to God should commence, by our being deeply convinced that all which happens to us moment by moment is the will of God, and therefore all that is necessary to us.

This conviction will render us contented with everything, and will make us see the commonest events in God, and not in the creature.

I beg of you, whoever you may be, who are desirous of giving yourselves to God, not to take yourselves back when once you are given to Him, and to remember that a thing once given away is no longer at your disposal. *Abandonment* is the key to the inner life: he who is thoroughly abandoned will soon be perfect.

You must, then, hold firmly to your abandonment, without listening to reason or to reflection. A great faith makes a great abandonment; you must trust wholly in God, against hope believing in hope (Rom. iv. 18). *Abandonment* is the casting off of all care of ourselves, to leave ourselves to be guided entirely by God.

All Christians are exhorted to abandonment, for it is said to all, "Take no thought for the morrow; for your Heavenly Father knoweth that ye have need of all these things" (Matt. vi. 32, 34). "In all thy ways acknowledge Him, and He shall direct thy paths" (Prov. iii. 6). "Commit thy works unto the Lord, and thy thoughts shall be established" (Prov. xvi. 3). "Commit thy way unto the Lord; trust also in Him; and He shall bring it to pass" (Ps. xxxvii. 5).

Abandonment, then, ought to be an utter leaving of ourselves, both outwardly and inwardly, in the hands of God, forgetting ourselves, and thinking only of God. By this means the heart is kept always free and contented.

Practically it should be a continual loss of our own will in the will of God, a renunciation of all natural inclinations, however good they may appear, in order that we may be left free to choose only as God chooses: we should be indifferent to all things, whether temporal or spiritual, for the body or the soul; leaving the past in forgetfulness, the future to providence, and giving the present to God; contented with the present moment, which brings with it God's eternal will for us; attributing nothing which happens to us to the creature, but seeing all things in God, and regarding them as coming infallibly from His hand, with the exception only of our own sin.

Leave yourselves, then, to be guided by God as He will, whether as regards the inner or the outward life.

CHAPTER VI

OF SUFFERING WHICH MUST BE ACCEPTED AS FROM GOD—ITS FRUITS.

Be content with all the suffering that God may lay upon you. If you will love Him purely, you will be as willing to follow Him to Calvary as to Tabor.

He must be loved as much on Calvary as on Tabor, since it is there that He makes the greatest manifestation of His love.

Do not act, then, like those people who give themselves at one time, and take themselves back at another. They give themselves to be caressed, and take themselves back when they are crucified; or else they seek for consolation in the creature.

You can only find consolation in the love of the cross and in complete abandonment. He who has no love for the cross has no love for God (see Matt. xvi. 24). It is impossible to love God without loving the cross; and a heart which has learned to love the cross finds sweetness, joy, and pleasure even in the bitterest things. "To the hungry soul every bitter thing is sweet" (Prov. xxvii. 7), because it is as hungry for the cross as it is hungry for God.

The cross gives God, and God gives the cross. Abandonment and the cross go together. As soon as you are sensible that something is repugnant to you which presents itself to you in the light of suffering, abandon yourself at once to God for that very thing, and present yourself as a sacrifice to Him: you will see that, when the cross comes, it will have lost much of its weight, because you will desire it. This will not prevent your being sensible of its weight. Some people imagine that it is not suffering to feel the cross. The feeling of suffering is one of the principal parts of suffering itself. Jesus Himself was willing to suffer it in its intensity.

Often the cross is borne with weakness, at other times with strength: all should be equal in the will of God.

CHAPTER VII
ON MYSTERIES—GOD GIVES THEM HERE IN REALITY.

It will be objected that, by this way, mysteries will not be made known. It is just the contrary; they are given to the soul in reality. Jesus Christ, to whom it is abandoned, and whom it follows as the *Way*, whom it hears as the *Truth*, and who animates it as the *Life*, impressing Himself upon it, imparts to it His own condition.

To bear the conditions of Christ is something far greater than merely to consider those conditions. Paul bore the conditions of Christ on his body. "I bear in my body," he says, "the marks of the Lord Jesus" (Gal. vi. 17). But he does not say that he reasoned about them.

Often Christ gives in this state of abandonment views of His conditions in a striking manner. We must receive equally all the dispositions in which He may be pleased to place us, choosing for ourselves to abide near to Him, and to be annihilated before Him, but receiving equally all that He gives us, light or dark-ness, facility or barrenness, strength or weakness, sweetness or bitterness, temptations or distractions, sorrow, care, uncertainty; none of these things ought to move us.

There are some persons to whom God is continually revealing His mysteries: let them be faithful to them. But when God sees fit to remove them, let them suffer them to be taken.

Others are troubled because no mysteries are made known to them: this is needless, since a loving attention to God includes all particular devotion, and that which is united to God alone, by its rest in Him, is instructed in a most excellent manner in all mysteries. He who loves God loves all that is of Him.

CHAPTER VIII

ON VIRTUE—ALL VIRTUES GIVEN WITH GOD IN THIS DEGREE OF THE PRAYER OF THE HEART.

This is the short and the sure way of acquiring virtue; because, God being the principle of all virtue, we possess all virtue in possessing God.

More than this, I say that all virtue which is not given inwardly is a mask of virtue, and like a garment that can be taken off, and will wear out. But virtue communicated fundamentally is essential, true, and permanent. "The King's daughter is all glorious within" (Ps. xlv. 13). And there are none who practise virtue more constantly than those who acquire it in this way, though virtue is not a distinct subject of their thought.

How hungry these loving ones are after suffering! They think only of what can please their Beloved, and they begin to neglect themselves, and to think less of themselves. The more they love God, the more they hate themselves.

Oh, if all could learn this method, so easy that it is suited for all, for the most ignorant as for the most learned, how easily the whole Church would be reformed! You only need to love. St Augustine says, "Love, and do as you please;" for when we love perfectly, we shall not desire to do anything that could be displeasing to our Beloved.

CHAPTER IX

OF PERFECT CONVERSION, WHICH IS AN
EFFECT OF THIS METHOD OF PRAYER—TWO
OF ITS AIDS, THE ATTRACTION OF GOD, AND
THE CENTRAL INCLINATION OF THE SOUL.

"Turn ye unto Him from whom the children of Israel have deeply revolted" (Isa. xxxi. 6). Conversion is nothing else but a turning from the creature to God. Conversion is not perfect, though it is necessary for salvation, when it is merely a turning from sin to grace. To be complete, it must be a turning from without to within.

The soul, being turned in the direction of God, has a great facility for remaining converted to Him. The longer it is converted, the nearer it approaches to God, and attaches itself to Him; and the nearer it approaches to God, the more it becomes necessarily drawn from the creature, which is opposed to God.

But this cannot be done by a violent effort of the creature; all that it can do is to remain turned in the direction of God in a perpetual adherence.

God has an *attracting virtue*, which draws the soul more strongly towards Himself; and in attracting it, He purifies it: as we see the sun attracting a dense vapour, and gradually, without any other effort on the part of the vapour than that of letting itself be drawn, the sun, by bringing it near to himself, refines and purifies it.

There is, however, this difference, that the vapour is not drawn freely, and does not follow willingly, as is the case with the soul.

This manner of turning within is very simple, and makes the soul advance naturally and without effort; because God is its centre. The centre has always a strong attractive power; and the larger the centre, the stronger is its attractive force.

Besides this attraction of the centre, there is given to all natural objects a strong tendency to become united with their centre. As soon as anything is turned in the direction of its centre, unless it be stopped by some invincible obstacle, it rushes towards it with extreme velocity. A stone in the air is no sooner let loose, and turned towards the earth, than it tends to it by its own weight as its centre. It is the same with fire and water, which, being no longer arrested, run incessantly towards their centre.

Now I say that the soul, by the effort it has made in inward recollection, being turned towards its centre, without any other effort, but simply by the weight of love, falls towards its centre; and the more it remains quiet and at rest, making no movement of its own, the more rapidly it will advance, because it thus allows that attractive virtue to draw it.

All the care, then, that we need have is to promote this inward recollection as much as possible, not being astonished at the difficulty we may find in this exercise, which will soon be recompensed with a wonderful co-operation on the part of God, which will render it very easy. When the passions rise, a look towards God, who is present within us, easily deadens them.

Any other resistance would irritate rather than appease
them.

CHAPTER X

HIGHER DEGREE OF PRAYER, WHICH IS THAT OF THE SIMPLE PRESENCE OF GOD, OR ACTIVE CONTEMPLATION.

The soul, faithfully exercising itself in the affection and love of its God, is astonished to find Him taking complete possession of it.

His presence becomes so natural, that it would be impossible not to have it: it becomes habitual to the soul, which is also conscious of a great calm spreading over it. Its prayer is all silence, and God imparts to it an intrinsic love, which is the commencement of ineffable happiness.

Oh, if I could describe the infinite degrees which follow! But I must stop here, since I am writing for beginners, and wait till God shall bring to light what may be useful to those more advanced.[1] I can only say, that, at this point, it is most important that all natural operation should cease, that God may act alone: "Be still, and know that I am God," is His own word by David (Ps. xlvi. 10).

But man is so attached to his own works, that he cannot believe God is working, unless he can feel, know, and distinguish His operation. He does not see that it is the speed of his course which prevents his seeing the extent of his advancement; and that the operation of God becoming more abundant, absorbs that

---

1   This subject is pursued in the treatise entitled "Spiritual Torrents."

of the creature, as we see that the sun, in proportion as he rises, absorbs the light of the stars, which were easily distinguishable before he appeared. It is not the want of light, but an excess of light, which prevents our distinguishing the stars.

It is the same here; man can no longer distinguish his own operation, because the strong light absorbs all his little distinct lights, and makes them fade away entirely, because God's excess surpasses them all. So that those who accuse this degree of prayer of being a state of *idleness*, are greatly deceived; and only speak thus from want of experience. Oh, if they would only prove it! in how short a time they would become experimentally acquainted with this matter!

I say, then, that this failure of work does not spring from scarcity, but from abundance.

Two classes of persons are silent: the one because they have nothing to say, the other because they have too much. It is thus in this degree. We are silent from excess, not from want.

Water causes death to two persons in very different ways. One dies of thirst, another is drowned: the one dies from want, the other from abundance. So here it is abundance which causes the cessation of natural operation. It is therefore important in this degree to remain as much as possible in stillness.

At the commencement of this prayer, a movement of affection is necessary; but when grace begins to flow into us, we have nothing to do but to remain at rest, and take all that God gives. Any other movement would prevent our profiting by this grace, which is given in order to draw us into the *rest of love*.

The soul in this peaceful attitude of prayer falls into a mystic sleep, in which all its natural powers are silenced, until that which had been temporary becomes its permanent condition. You see that the soul is thus led, without effort, without study, without artifice.

The heart is not a fortified place, which must be taken by cannonading and violence: it is a kingdom of peace, which is possessed by love. Gently following in His train, you will soon reach the degree of *intuitive* prayer. God asks nothing extraordinary and difficult: on the contrary, He is most pleased with childlike simplicity.

The grandest part of religion is the most simple. It is the same with natural things. Do you wish to get to the sea? Embark upon a river, and insensibly and without effort you will be taken to it. Do you wish to get to God? Take His way, so quiet, so easy, and in a little while you will be taken to Him in a manner that will surprise you. Oh, if only you would try it! How soon you would see that I am telling you only too little, and that the experience would far surpass any description that could be given! What do you fear? Why do you not throw yourself at once into the arms of Love, who only stretched them out upon the cross in order to take you in? What risk can there be in trusting God, and abandoning yourself to Him? Oh, He will not deceive you, unless it be by giving you far more than you ever expected: while those who expect everything from themselves may well take to themselves the reproach which God utters by the mouth of Isaiah: "Thou art wearied in the greatness of thy way; yet saidst thou not, There is no hope" (Isa. lvii. 10).

CHAPTER XI

OF REST IN THE PRESENCE OF GOD— ITS FRUITS—INWARD SILENCE—GOD COMMANDS IT—OUTWARD SILENCE.

The soul, being brought to this place, needs no other preparation than that of repose: for *the presence of God* during the day, which is the great result of prayer, or rather prayer itself, begins to be *intuitive* and *almost continual.* The soul is conscious of a deep inward happiness, and feels that God is in it more truly than it is in itself. It has only one thing to do in order to find God, which is to retire within itself. As soon as the eyes are closed, it finds itself in prayer.

It is astonished at this infinite happiness; there is carried on within it a conversation which outward things cannot interrupt. It might be said of this method of prayer, as was said of Wisdom, "All good things together come to me with her" (Wisdom of Solomon vii. 11), for virtue flows naturally into the soul, and is practised so easily, that it seems to be quite natural to it. It has within it a germ of life and fruitfulness, which gives it a facility for all good, and an insensibility to all evil. Let it then remain faithful, and seek no other frame of mind than that of simple rest. It has only to suffer itself to be filled with this divine effusion.

"The Lord is in His holy temple: let all the earth keep silence before Him" (Hab. ii. 20). The reason why inward silence is so necessary is, that Christ, being the eternal and essential Word, in order that He may be received into the soul, there must be a disposition corresponding with what He is. Now it is certain that in order to receive words we must listen. Hearing is the sense given to enable us to receive the words which are communicated to us. Hearing is rather a passive than an active sense, receiving, and not communicating. Christ being the Word which is to be communicated, the soul must be attentive to this Word which speaks within it.

This is why we are so often exhorted to listen to God, and to be attentive to His voice. Many passages might be quoted. I will be content to mention a few: "Hearken unto me, O my people; and give ear unto me, O my nation" (Isa. li. 4). "Hearken unto me, O house of Jacob, and all the remnant of the house of Israel" (Isa. xlvi. 31). "Hearken, O daughter, and consider, and incline thine ear; forget also thine own people, and thy father's house; so shall the King greatly desire thy beauty" (Ps. xlv. 10, 11).

We must *listen* to God, and be attentive to Him, *forgetting ourselves* and all self-interest. These two actions, or rather passions—for this condition is essentially a passive one—arouse in God a "desire" towards the "beauty" He has Himself communicated.

Outward silence is extremely necessary for the cultivation of inward silence, and it is impossible to acquire inward silence without having a love for silence and solitude.

God tells us by the mouth of His prophet, "I will allure her, and bring her into the wilderness, and speak to her heart" (marginal reading of Hosea ii. 14).

To be inwardly occupied with God, and outwardly occupied with countless trifles, this is impossible.

It will be a small matter to pray, and to retire within ourselves for half an hour or an hour, if we do not retain the unction and the spirit of prayer during the day.

CHAPTER XII

SELF-EXAMINATION AND CONFESSION.

Self-examination should always precede confession. Those who arrive at this degree should expose themselves to God, who will not fail to enlighten them, and to make known to them the nature of their faults. This examination must be conducted in peace and tranquillity, expecting more from God than from our own research the knowledge of our sins.

When we examine ourselves with an effort, we easily make mistakes. We "call evil good, and good evil;" and self-esteem easily deceives us. But when we remain exposed to the searching gaze of God, that Divine Sun brings to light even the smallest atoms. We must then, for self-examination, abandon ourselves utterly to God.

When we are in this degree of prayer, God is not slow to reveal to us all the faults we commit. We have no sooner sinned than we feel a burning reproach.

It is God Himself who conducts an examination which nothing escapes, and we have only to turn towards God, and suffer the pain and the correction which He gives. As this examination by God is continual, we can no longer examine ourselves; and if we are faithful to our abandonment to God, we shall soon be better examined by the divine light than we could be by all our own efforts. Experience will make this known. One thing which often causes astonishment to the soul is, that when it is conscious of a sin, and comes to confess it to God, instead of feeling regret and contrition, such as it formerly felt, a sweet and gentle love takes possession of it.

Not having experienced this before, it supposes that it ought to draw itself out of this condition to make a definite act of contrition. But it does not see that, by doing this, it would lose true contrition, which is this *intuitive love*, infinitely greater than anything it could create for itself. It is a higher action, which includes the others, with greater perfection, though these are not possessed distinctly.

We should not seek to do anything for ourselves when God acts more excellently in us and for us. It is hating sin as God hates it to hate it in this way. This love, which is the operation of God in the soul, is the purest of all love. All we have to do then is to remain as we are.

Another remarkable thing is, that we often forget our faults, and find it difficult to remember them; but this must not trouble us, for two reasons: The first, that this very forgetfulness is a proof that the sin has been atoned for, and it is better to forget all that concerns ourselves, that we may remember God alone. The second reason is, that God does not fail, whenever confession is needful, to show to the soul its greatest faults, for then it is He Himself who examines it.

CHAPTER XIII

ON READING — VOCAL PRAYER — REQUESTS.

The proper manner of reading in this degree is, as soon as we feel attracted to meditation, to cease reading, and remain at rest.

The soul is no sooner called to inward silence, than it should cease to utter vocal prayers; saying but little at any time, and when it does say them, if it finds any difficulty, or feels itself drawn to silence, it should remain silent, and make no effort to pray, leaving itself to the guidance of the Spirit of God.

The soul will find that it cannot, as formerly, present definite requests to God. This need not surprise it, for it is now that "the Spirit maketh intercession for the saints, according to the will of God. The Spirit also helpeth our infirmities: for we know not what we should pray for as we ought; but the Spirit itself maketh intercession for us, with groanings which cannot be uttered" (Rom. viii. 26, 27).

We must second the designs of God, which are to strip the soul of its own works, to substitute His in their place.

Let Him work then, and bind yourself to nothing of your own. However good it may appear to you, it cannot be so if it comes in the way of God's will for you. The will of God is preferable to all other good. Seek not your own interests, but live by abandonment and by faith.

It is here that *faith* begins to operate wonderfully in the soul.

CHAPTER XIV

THE FAULTS COMMITTED IN THIS DEGREE — DISTRACTIONS, TEMPTATIONS — THE COURSE TO BE PURSUED RESPECTING THEM.

As soon as we fall into a fault, or have wandered, we must turn again within ourselves; because this fault having turned us from God, we should as soon as possible turn towards Him, and suffer the penitence which He Himself will give.

It is of great importance that we should not be anxious about these faults, because the anxiety only springs from a secret pride and a love of our own excellence. We are troubled at feeling what we are.

If we become discouraged, we shall grow weaker yet; and reflection upon our faults produces a vexation which is worse than the sin itself.

A truly humble soul does not marvel at its weakness, and the more it perceives its wretchedness, the more it abandons itself to God, and seeks to remain near to Him, knowing how deeply it needs His help. God's own word to us is, "I will instruct thee, and teach thee in the way which thou shalt go: I will guide thee with mine eye" (Ps. xxxii. 8).

In distractions or temptations, instead of combating them directly, which would only serve to augment them, and to wean us from God, with whom alone we ought to be occupied, we should simply turn away from them, and draw nearer to God; as a little child, seeing a fierce animal approaching it, would not stay to fight it, nor even to look at it, but would run for shelter to its mother's arms, where it would be safe. "God is in the midst of her, she shall not be moved: God shall help her, and that right early" (Ps. xlvi. 5).

If we adopt any other course of action, if we attempt to attack our enemies in our weakness, we shall be wounded, even if we are not entirely defeated; but remaining in the simple presence of God, we find ourselves immediately fortified.

This was what David did: he says, "I have set the Lord always before me; because He is at my right hand, I shall not be moved. Therefore my heart is glad, and my glory rejoiceth; my flesh also shall rest in hope." It is also said by Moses, "The Lord shall fight for you, and ye shall hold your peace" (Exod. xiv. 14).

CHAPTER XV

PRAYER AND SACRIFICE EXPLAINED BY
THE SIMILITUDE OF A PERFUME—OUR
ANNIHILATION IN THIS SACRIFICE—
SOLIDITY AND FRUITFULNESS OF THIS
PRAYER AS SET FORTH IN THE GOSPEL.

Prayer ought to be both petition and sacrifice.

Prayer, according to the testimony of St John, is an incense, whose perfume rises to God. Therefore it is said in the Revelation (chap. viii. 3), that an angel held a censer, which contained the incense of the prayers of saints.

Prayer is an outpouring of the heart in the presence of God. "I have poured out my soul before the Lord," said the mother of Samuel (1 Sam. i. 15). Thus the prayers of the Magi at the feet of the infant Jesus in the stable of Bethlehem were signified by the incense which they offered.

Prayer is the heat of love, which melts and dissolves the soul, and carries it to God. In proportion as it melts, it gives out its odour, and this odour comes from the love which burns it.

This is what the Bride meant when she said, "While the King sitteth at His table, my spikenard sendeth forth the smell thereof" (Cant. i. 12). The table is the heart. When God is there, and we are kept near to Him, in His presence, this presence of God melts and dissolves the hardness of our hearts, and as they melt, they give forth their perfume. Therefore the Bridegroom, seeing

His Bride thus melted by the speech of her Beloved, says, "Who is this that cometh out of the wilderness, perfumed with myrrh and frankincense?" (Cant. iii. 6).

Thus the soul rises up towards its God. But in order to this, it must suffer itself to be destroyed and annihilated by the force of love. This is a state of *sacrifice* essential to the Christian religion, by which the soul suffers itself to be destroyed and annihilated to render homage to the sovereignty of God; as it is written, "The power of the Lord is great, and He is honoured of the lowly" (Ecclus. iii. 20). And the destruction of our own being confesses the sovereign being of God.

We must cease to be, so that the Spirit of the Word may be in us. In order that He may come to us, we must yield our life to Him, and die to self that He may live in us, and that we being dead, our life may be hidden with Christ in God (Col. iii. 3).

"Come unto me," says God, "all ye that be desirous of me, and fill yourselves with my fruits" (Ecclus. xxiv. 19). But how can we be filled with God? Only by being emptied of self, and going out of ourselves in order to be lost in Him.

Now, this can never be brought about except by our becoming nothing. Nothingness is true prayer, which renders to God "honour, and glory, and power, for ever and ever" (Rev. v. 13).

This prayer is the prayer of truth. It is worshipping the Father in spirit and in truth. In *spirit*, because we are by it drawn out of our human and carnal action, to enter into the purity of the Spirit, who prays in us; and in *truth*, because the soul is led into the truth of the ALL of God, and the NOTHING of the creature.

There are but these two truths, the ALL and the NOTHING. All the rest is untruth.

We can only honour the ALL of God by our NOTHINGNESS; and we have no sooner become nothing, than God, who will not suffer us to be empty, fills us with Himself. Oh, if all knew the blessings which come to the soul by this prayer, they would be satisfied with no others: it is the pearl of great price; it is the hidden treasure. He who finds it gladly sells all that he has to buy it (Matt. xiii. 44, 46). It is the well of living water, which springs up into everlasting life (John iv. 14). It is the practice of the pure maxims of the gospel.

Does not Christ Himself tell us that the kingdom of God is within us? (Luke xvii. 21). This kingdom is set up in two ways. The first is, when God is so thoroughly master of us that nothing resists Him: then our heart is truly His kingdom. The other way is, that by possessing God, who is the sovereign Lord, we possess the kingdom of God, which is the height of felicity, and the end for which we were created. As it has been said, *to serve God is to reign.*

The end for which we were created is to enjoy God in this life, and men do not believe it!

CHAPTER XVI

THIS STATE OF PRAYER NOT ONE OF IDLENESS, BUT OF NOBLE ACTION, WROUGHT BY THE SPIRIT OF GOD, AND IN DEPENDENCE UPON HIM—THE COMMUNICATION OF HIS LIFE AND UNION.

Some people, hearing of the prayer of silence, have wrongly imagined that the soul remains *inactive, lifeless*, and *without movement*.

But the truth is, that its action is more noble and more extensive than it ever was before it entered this degree, since it is moved by God Himself, and acted upon by His Spirit. St Paul desires that we should be *led by the Spirit of God* (Rom. viii. 14). I do not say that there must be no action, but that we must act in dependence upon the divine movement. This is admirably set forth by Ezekiel. The prophet saw wheels which had the spirit of life, and wherever this spirit was to go, they went; they went on, or stood, or were lifted up, as they were moved, for the spirit of life was in them: but they never went back (see Ezek. i. 19–21). It should be the same with the soul: it should suffer itself to be moved and guided by the living Spirit who is in it, following His direction, and no other. Now this Spirit will never lead it to go backwards, that is, to reflect upon the creature, or to lean upon itself, but always to go forward, pressing continually towards the mark.

This action of the soul is a restful action. When it acts of itself, it acts with effort; and is therefore more conscious of its action. But when it acts in dependence upon the Spirit of grace, its action is so free, so easy, so natural, that it does not seem to act at all. "He brought me forth also into a large place; He delivered me, because He delighted in me" (Ps. xviii. 19).

As soon as the soul has commenced its course towards its centre,[2] from that moment its action becomes vigorous—that is, its course towards the centre which attracts it, which infinitely surpasses the velocity of any other movement.

It is action then, but an action so *noble*, so *peaceful*, so *tranquil*, that it seems to the soul as though it were not acting at all; because it rests, as it were, naturally. When a wheel is only turning with a moderate speed, it can easily be distinguished; but when it goes quickly, no part of it can be distinctly seen. So the soul which remains at rest in God has an action infinitely noble and exalted, yet very peaceful. The greater its peace, the greater is its velocity, because it is abandoned to the Spirit, who moves it and makes it act. This Spirit is God Himself, who draws us, and in drawing makes us run to Him, as the Bride well knew when she said, "Draw me, we will run" (Cant. i. 4). Draw me, O my Divine Centre, by my inmost heart: my powers and my sensibilities will run at Thy attraction! This attraction alone is a balm which heals me, and a perfume which draws. "We will run," she says, "because of the savour of Thy good ointments." This attracting virtue is *very strong* but the soul follows it *very gladly*; and as it is

_____

2   See chap. ix.

equally strong and sweet, it attracts by its strength and delights by its sweetness.

The Bride says, "Draw me, we will run." She speaks of herself, and to herself: "Draw *me;*" there is the unity of the object which is attracted: "*We* will run;" there is the correspondence of all the powers and sensibilities which follow in the train of the centre of the heart.

It is not then a question of remaining in idleness, but of acting *in dependence upon the Spirit of God,* who animates us, since it is in Him that "we live, and move, and have our being" (Acts xvii. 23). This calm dependence upon the Spirit of God is absolutely necessary, and causes the soul in a short time to attain the simplicity and unity in which it was created. It was created one and simple, like God. In order, then, to answer the end of our creation, we must quit the multiplicity of our own actions, to enter into the simplicity and unity of God, in whose image we were created (Gen. i. 27). The Spirit of God is "one only," "yet manifold" (Wisdom of Solomon vii. 22), and its unity does not prevent its multiplicity. We enter into God's unity when we are united to His Spirit, because then we have the same Spirit that He has; and we are multiplied outwardly, as regards His dispositions, without leaving the unity.

So that, as God acts infinitely, and we are of one spirit with Him, we act much more than we could do by our own action. We must suffer ourselves to be guided by Wisdom. This "Wisdom" is more moving than any motion (Wisdom of Solomon vii. 24). Let us, then, remain in dependence upon His action, and our action will be vigorous indeed.

"All things were made by (the Word); and without Him was not anything made that was made" (John i. 3). God, in creating us, created us in His image, after His likeness (Gen. i. 26). He gave to us the Spirit of the Word by the breath of life (Gen. ii. 7), which He breathed into us when we were created in the image of God, by the participation of the life of the Word, who is the image of His Father. Now this life is one, simple, pure, intimate, and fruitful.

The devil having disfigured this beautiful image, it became necessary that this same Word, whose breath had been breathed into us at our creation, should come to restore it. It was necessary that it should be He, because He is the image of the Father; and a defaced image cannot be repaired by its own action, but by the action of him who seeks to restore it. Our *action* then should be, to *put ourselves* into a position to suffer the action of God, and to allow the Word to retrace His image in us. An image, if it could move, would by its movement prevent the sculptor's perfecting it. Every movement of our own hinders the work of the Heavenly Sculptor, and produces false features.

We must then remain silent, and only move as He moves us. Jesus Christ has *life in Himself* (John v. 26), and He must communicate life to all who live.

That this action is the most noble cannot be denied. Things are only of value as the principle in which they originate is noble, grand, and elevated. Actions committed by a divine principle are *divine actions*; whereas the actions of the creature, however good they may appear, are *human actions* or at best they are virtuous actions, if they are done with the help of grace.

Jesus says that He has life in Himself; all other beings have but a borrowed life, but the Word has life in Himself; and as He is communicative, He desires to communicate this life to men. We must then give place to this life, that it may flow in us, which can only be done by evacuation, and the loss of the life of Adam and of our own action, as St Paul assures us: "If any man be in Christ, he is a new creature: old things are passed away; behold all things are become new" (2 Cor. v. 17). This can only be brought about by the death of ourselves and of our own action, that the action of God may be substituted for it. We do not profess, then, to be without action, but only to act in dependence upon the Spirit of God, suffering His action to take the place of our own. Jesus shows us this in the gospel. Martha did good things, but because she did them of her own spirit, Christ reproved her for them. The spirit of man is turbulent and boisterous; therefore it does little, though it appears to do much. "Martha, Martha," said Jesus, "thou art careful and troubled about many things; but one thing is needful; and Mary hath chosen that good part, which shall not be taken away from her" (Luke x. 41, 42).

What had she chosen, this Magdalene? Peace, tranquillity, and repose. She apparently ceased to act, that she might be moved by the Spirit of God; she ceased to live, that Christ might live in her.

This is why it is so necessary to renounce ourselves and all our own works to follow Jesus; for we cannot follow Him unless we are animated with His Spirit. In order that the Spirit of Christ may dwell in us, our own spirit must give place to Him. "He that is joined to the Lord," says St Paul, "is one spirit" (1 Cor. vi. 17). "It is good for me to draw near to God: I have put my trust in the Lord God" (Ps. lxxiii. 28). What is this "drawing near"? It is the beginning of union.

Union has its beginning, its continuation, its completion, and its consummation. The commencement of union is an inclination towards God. When the soul is converted in the manner I have described, it has an inclination to its centre, and a strong tendency to union: this tendency is the commencement. Then it adheres, which happens when it approaches nearer to God; then it is united to Him, and finally becomes one with Him—that is, it becomes one spirit with Him; and it is then that this spirit, which proceeded from God, returns to Him as its end.

It is, then, necessary that we should enter this way, which is the divine motion, and the Spirit of Jesus Christ. St Paul says, "If any man have not the Spirit of Christ, he is none of His" (Rom. viii. 9). To be Christ's, then, we must suffer ourselves to be filled with His Spirit, and emptied of our own: our hearts must be evacuated. St Paul, in the same place, proves to us the necessity of this divine motion: he says, "As many as are led by the Spirit of God, they are the sons of God" (Rom. viii. 14).

The divinely-imparted Spirit is the Spirit of divine sonship; therefore, the same apostle continues, "Ye have not received the spirit of bondage again to fear; but ye have received the spirit of adoption, whereby we cry, Abba, Father" (Rom. viii. 15). This spirit is no other than the Spirit of Christ, by whom we participate in His Sonship; and this "Spirit itself beareth witness with our spirit that we are the sons of God."

As soon as the soul leaves itself to be moved by the Spirit of God, it experiences the witness of this divine sonship; and this witness serves the more to increase its joy, as it makes it know *that it is called to the liberty of the sons of God*, and that the spirit it has received is not a spirit of bondage, but of liberty.

The Spirit of the divine motion is so necessary for all things, that Paul founds this necessity upon our ignorance of the things that we ask for. "The Spirit," he says, "helpeth our infirmities; for we know not what we should pray for as we ought; but the Spirit itself maketh intercession for us, with groanings which cannot be uttered." This is conclusive: if we do not know what to pray for, nor how to ask as we ought for what is necessary for us, and if it is needful that the Spirit who is in us, to whose motion we abandon ourselves, should ask it for us, ought we not to leave Him to do it? He does it "with groanings which cannot be uttered."

This Spirit is the Spirit of the Word, who is always heard, as He says Himself: "I know that Thou hearest me always" (John xi. 42). If we leave it to the Spirit within us to ask and to pray, we shall always be answered. Why so? O great apostle, mystic teacher, so deeply taught in the inner life! teach us why. "It is," he adds, "because He that searcheth the hearts knoweth what is the mind of the Spirit, because He maketh intercession for the saints according to the will of God;" that is to say, this Spirit only asks that which it is God's will to give. It is God's will that we should be saved and that we should be perfect. He asks, then, for all that is necessary to our perfection. Why, after this, should we be burdened with superfluous cares, and be wearied in the greatness of our way, without ever saying, There is no hope in ourselves, and therefore resting in God? God Himself invites us to cast all our care upon Him, and He complains, in inconceivable goodness, that we employ our strength, our riches, and our treasure, in countless exterior things, although there is so little joy to be found in them all. "Wherefore do ye spend money for that which is not bread, and your labour for that which satisfieth not? Hearken diligently unto me, and eat ye that which is good, and let your soul delight itself in fatness" (Isa. lv. 2).

Oh, if it were known what happiness there is in thus hearkening unto God, and how the soul is strengthened by it! All flesh must be silent before the Lord (see Zech. ii. 13). All self-effort must cease when He appears. In order still further to induce us to abandon ourselves to Him without reserve, God assures us that we need fear nothing from such abandonment, because He has a special individual care over each of us. He says, "Can a woman forget her sucking-child, that she should not have compassion on the son of her womb? Yea, she may forget, yet will I not forget thee" (Isa. xlix. 15). Ah, words full of consolation! Who on hearing them can fear to abandon himself utterly to the guidance of God?

CHAPTER XVII

DISTINCTION BETWEEN EXTERIOR AND
INTERIOR ACTIONS—THOSE OF THE SOUL
IN THIS CONDITION ARE INTERIOR,
BUT HABITUAL, CONTINUED, DIRECT,
PROFOUND, SIMPLE, AND IMPERCEPTIBLE—
BEING A CONTINUAL SINKING IN THE
OCEAN OF DIVINITY—SIMILITUDE
OF A VESSEL—HOW TO ACT IN THE
ABSENCE OF SENSIBLE SUPPORTS.

The actions of men are either exterior or interior. The *exterior* are those which appear outwardly, and have a sensible object, possessing neither good nor evil qualities, excepting as they receive them from the interior principle in which they originate. It is not of these that I intend to speak, but only of interior actions, which are those actions of the soul by which it *applies itself* inwardly to some object, or *turns away* from some other.

When, being applied to God, I desire to commit an action of a different nature from those which He would prompt, I turn away from God, and I turn towards created things more or less according to the strength or weakness of my action. If, being turned towards the creature, I wish to return to God, I must commit the action of turning away from the creature, and turning towards God; and thus the more perfect is this action, the more complete will be the conversion.

Until I am perfectly converted, I need several actions

to turn me towards God. Some are done all at once, others gradually; but my action ought to lead me to turn to God, employing all the strength of my soul for Him, as it is written, "Therefore even now, saith the Lord, turn ye even to me with all your heart" (Joel ii. 12). "Thou shalt return unto the Lord thy God ... with all thine heart and with all thy soul" (Deut. xxx. 2). God only asks for our heart: "My son, give me thy heart, and let thine eyes observe my ways" (Prov. xxiii. 26). To give the heart to God is to have its gaze, its strength, and its vigour all centred in Him, to follow His will. We must, then, after we have applied to God, remain always turned towards Him.

But as the mind of man is weak, and the soul, being accustomed to turn towards earthly things, is easily turned away from God, it must, as soon as it perceives that it is turned towards outward things, resume its former position in God by a simple act of return to Him.

And as several repeated acts form a habit, the soul contracts a habit of conversion, and from action it passes to a habitual condition.

The soul, then, must not seek by means of any efforts or works of its own to come near to God; this is seeking to perform one action by means of others, instead of by a simple action remaining attached to God alone.

If we believe that we must commit no actions, we are mistaken, for *we are always acting*; but each one must act according to his degree.

I will endeavour to make this point clear, as, for

want of understanding it, it presents a difficulty to many Christians.

There are *passing* and *distinct* actions, and *continued* actions; *direct* acts and *reflected* acts. All cannot perform the first, and all are not in a condition to perform the others. The first actions should be committed by those who are turned away from God. They ought to turn to Him by a distinct action, more or less strong according to their distance from Him.

By a *continued* action I understand that by which the soul is completely turned towards its God by a *direct* action, which it does not renew, unless it has been interrupted, but which exists. The soul being altogether turned in this way, is in love, and remains there: "And he that dwelleth in love, dwelleth in God" (1 John iv. 16). Then the soul may be said to be in a habitual act, resting even in this action. But its rest is not idle, for it has an action *always in force,* viz., *a gentle sinking in God,* in which God attracts it more and more strongly; and, following this attraction, and resting in love, it sinks more and more in this love, and has an action infinitely stronger, more vigorous, and more prompt, than that action which forms only the return. Now the soul which is in this *profound and strong action,* being turned towards its God, does not perceive this action, because it is direct, and not reflex; so that persons in this condition, not knowing how rightly to describe it, say that *they have no action.* But they are mistaken; they were never more active. It would be better to say they do not distinguish any action, than that they do not commit any.

The soul does not act of itself, I admit; but it is drawn, and it follows the attracting power. Love is the weight which sinks it, as a person who falls in the sea sinks, and would sink to infinity if the sea were infinite; and without perceiving its sinking, it would sink to the most profound depths with an incredible speed. It is, then, incorrect to say that no actions are committed. All commit actions, but all do not commit them in the same manner; and the abuse arises from the fact, that those who know that action is inevitable wish it to be *distinct* and *sensible*. But sensible action is for beginners, and the other for those more advanced. To stop with the first would be to deprive ourselves of the last; and to wish to commit the last before having passed the first would be an equal abuse.

Everything must be done in its season; each state has its commencement, its progress, and its end. There is no act which has not its beginning. At first we must work with *effort*, but afterwards we enjoy the fruit of our labour.

When a vessel is in the harbour, the sailors have a difficulty in bringing it into the open sea; but once there, they easily turn it in the direction in which they wish to navigate. So, when the soul is in sin, it needs an effort to drag it out; the cords which bind it must be loosened; then, by means of strong and vigorous action, it must be drawn within itself, little by little leaving the harbour, and being turned within, which is the place to which its voyage should be directed.

When the vessel is thus turned, in proportion as it advances in the sea, it leaves the land behind it, and the further it goes from the land, the less effort is needed to carry it along. At last it begins to sail gently, and the vessel goes on so rapidly that the oars become useless. What does the pilot do then? He is contented with spreading the sails and sitting at the helm.

Spreading the sails is simply laying ourselves before God, to be moved by His Spirit. *Sitting at the helm* is preventing our heart from leaving the right way, rowing it gently, and leading it according to the movement of the Spirit of God, who gradually takes possession of it, as the wind gradually fills the sails, and impels the vessel forward. So long as the vessel sails before the wind, the mariners rest from their labour. They voyage farther in an hour, while they rest in this manner and leave the ship to be carried along by the wind, than they would in a much longer time by their own efforts; and if they wished to row, besides the fatigue which would result from it, their labour would be useless, and would only serve to retard the vessel.

This is the conduct we should pursue in our inner life, and in acting thus we shall advance more in a short time by the Divine guidance, than we ever could do by our own efforts. If only you will try this way, you will find it the easiest possible.

When the wind is contrary, if the wind and the tempest are violent, the anchor must be thrown in the sea to stop the vessel. This *anchor* is trust in God and hope in His goodness, waiting in patience for the tempest to cease, and for a favourable wind to return, as David did: "I waited patiently for the Lord," he says, "and He inclined unto me" (Ps. xl. 1).

CHAPTER XVIII

THE DRYNESS OF PREACHERS, AND THE
VARIOUS EVILS WHICH ARISE FROM
THEIR FAILING TO TEACH HEART-
PRAYER—EXHORTATION TO PASTORS TO
LEAD PEOPLE TOWARDS THIS FORM OF
PRAYER, WITHOUT AMUSING THEM WITH
STUDIED AND METHODICAL DEVOTION.

If all those who are working for the conquest of souls sought to win them *by the heart*, leading them first of all to prayer and to the inner life, they would see many and lasting conversions. But so long as they only address themselves to the outside, and instead of drawing people to Christ by occupying their hearts with Him, they only give them a thousand precepts for outward observances, they will see but little fruit, and that will not be lasting.

When once the heart is won, other defects are easily corrected. This is why God particularly asks for the *heart*. By this means alone would be prevented the drunkenness, blasphemy, lewdness, enmity, and robbery which are prevalent in the world. Jesus Christ would reign universally, and the Church everywhere would be revived.

Error only takes possession of the soul in the absence of faith and prayer. If men could be taught to *believe simply* and to *pray*, instead of disputing amongst themselves, they would be gently led to Christ.

Oh, how inestimable is the loss of those who neglect

the inner life! Oh, what an account will they have to render to God who have the charge of souls, for not having discovered this hidden treasure to all those whom they serve in the ministry of the Word!

The excuse given is that there is *danger* in this way, or that ignorant people are incapable of spiritual things. The oracle of truth assures us that God has hid these things from the wise and prudent, and has revealed them to babes. And what danger can there be in walking in the only true way, which is Jesus Christ, in giving ourselves to Him, looking to Him continually, putting all our trust in His grace, and tending, with all the forces of our souls, to His pure love?

Far from the simple ones being *incapable* of this perfection, they are the most suitable for it, because they are more docile, more humble, and more innocent; and as they do not reason, they are not so attached to their own light. Having no science, they more readily suffer themselves to be guided by the Spirit of God: while others who are blind in their own sufficiency resist the divine inspiration.

God tells us, too, that it is to the *simple* He gives understanding by the entrance of His Word (Ps. cxix. 130). "The testimony of the Lord is sure, making wise the *simple*" (Ps. xix. 7). "The Lord preserveth the *simple*: I was brought low, and He helped me" (Ps. cxvi. 6).

O ye who have the oversight of souls! see that you do not prevent the little ones from going to Christ. His words to His disciples were, "Suffer little children to come unto me, and forbid them not; for of such is the kingdom of God" (Luke xviii. 16). Jesus only said this to His disciples, because they wished to keep the children away from Him. Often the remedy is applied to the body, when the disease is at the *heart*. The reason why we have so little success in seeking to reform men, is that we direct our efforts to the outside, and all that we can do there soon passes off. But if we were to give them first *the key of the interior*, the outside would be reformed at once with a natural facility.

And this is very easy. To teach them to seek God in their heart, to think of Him, to return to Him when they find they have turned away, to do all and suffer all for the sake of pleasing Him—this is to direct them to the source of all grace, and to make them find there all that is necessary for their sanctification. O you who serve souls! I conjure you to put them first of all into this way, which is Jesus Christ; and it is He who conjures you to do this by the blood He has shed for the souls He confides to your care. "Speak to the heart of Jerusalem" (Isa. xl. 2, marg.) O dispensers of His grace, preachers of His Word, ministers of sacraments! establish His kingdom; and, in order to establish it truly, make it reign over HEARTS. For as it is the heart alone which can oppose His empire, it is by the subjection of the heart that His sovereignty is most honoured. Alas! we seek to make *studied* prayers; and by wishing to arrange them too much, we render them impossible. We have alienated children from the best of Fathers, in seeking to teach them a polished language.

Go, poor children, and speak to your Heavenly Father in your natural language: however uncultivated it may be, it is not so to Him. A father loves best the speech which is put in disorder by love and respect, because he sees that it comes from the heart: it is more to him than a dry harangue, vain and unfruitful though well studied. Oh, how certain glances of love charm and ravish Him! They express infinitely more than all language and reason. By wishing to teach how to love Love Himself with method, much of this love has been lost. Oh! it is not necessary to teach the art of loving. The language of love is barbarous to him who does not love; and we cannot learn to love God better than by loving Him. The Spirit of God does not need our arrangements; He takes shepherds at His pleasure to make them prophets; and, far from closing the palace of prayer to any, as it is imagined, He leaves the doors open to all, and Wisdom is ordered to cry in the public places, "Whoso is simple, let him turn in hither: as for him that wanteth understanding, she saith to him, Come, eat of my bread, and drink of the wine which I have mingled" (Prov. ix. 4, 5). Did not Christ thank His Father that He had hidden these things from the wise and prudent, and had revealed them to babes? (Matt. xi. 25.)

CHAPTER XIX

AFTER THE PRECEDING WAYS, THERE
REMAINS AN AFTER WAY, PREPARATORY
TO DIVINE UNION, IN WHICH WISDOM AND
JUSTICE MAKE THE PASSIVE PURIFICATION
OF THE SOUL, ALL WHICH IS TREATED
IN DETAIL IN THE FOLLOWING TREATISE,
ENTITLED "SPIRITUAL TORRENTS."

It is impossible to attain divine union by the way of meditation alone, or even by the affections, or by any luminous or understood prayer. There are several reasons. These are the principal.

First, according to Scripture, "No man shall see God and live" (Exod. xxxiii. 20). Now all discursive exercises of prayer, or even of *active contemplation*, regarded as an end, and not as a preparation for the *passive*, are exercises of life by which we cannot see God, that is, become united to Him. All that is of man, and of his own industry, however noble and elevated it may be, must die.

St John tells us that "there was silence in heaven." Heaven represents the depths and centre of the soul, where all must be in silence when the majesty of God appears. All that belongs to our own efforts, or to ourselves in any way, must be destroyed, because nothing is opposed to God but appropriation, and all the malignity of man is in this appropriation, which is the source of his evil; so that the more a soul loses its appropriation, the more it becomes pure.

Secondly, in order to unite two things so opposed as the purity of God and the impurity of the creature, the simplicity of God and the multiplicity of the creature, God must operate alone; for this can never be done by the effort of the creature, since two things cannot be united unless there is some relation or resemblance between them, as an impure metal would never unite with one that was pure and refined.

What does God do then? He sends before Him His own Wisdom, as fire will be sent upon the earth to consume by its activity all the impurity that is there. Fire consumes all things, and nothing resists its activity. It is the same with Wisdom; it consumes all impurity in the creature, to prepare him for divine union.

This impurity, so opposed to union, is appropriation and activity. *Appropriation*, because it is the source of the real impurity which can never be united to essential purity; as the sun's rays may touch the mud but cannot unite with it. *Activity*, because God being in an infinite repose, in order that the soul may be united to Him, it must participate in His repose, without which there can be no union, because of the dissemblance; and to unite two things, they must be in a proportionate rest.

It is for this reason that the soul can only attain divine union by the rest of its will; and it can only be united to God when it is in a *central rest* and in the purity of its creation.

To purify the soul God makes use of wisdom as fire is used for the purification of gold. It is certain that gold can only be purified by fire, which gradually consumes all that is earthly and foreign, and separates it from the gold. It is not sufficient that the earth should be changed into gold; it is necessary that the fire should melt and dissolve it, to remove from it all that is earthly; and this gold is put in the fire so many times that it loses its impurity, and all necessity of purification. Then it is fit to be employed in the most excellent workmanship.

And if this gold is impure in the end, it is because it has contracted fresh defilement by coming in contact with other bodies. But this impurity is only superficial, and does not prevent its being used; whereas its former impurity was hidden within it, and, as it were, identified with its nature.

In addition to this, you will remark that gold of an inferior degree of purity cannot mix with that of a superior purity. The one must contract the impurity of the other, or else impart its own purity to it. Put a refined gold with an unrefined one, what can the gold-smith ever do with it? He will have all the impurity taken from the second piece, that it may be able to mix with the first. This is what St Paul tells us, that "the fire shall try every man's work of what sort it is;" he adds, that if any man's work should be found to deserve burning, he should be saved "so as by fire" (1 Cor. iii. 13, 15). That means, that though there are some works which are good, and which God receives, yet, so that he who has done them may be pure, they too must pass through the fire, in order that all appropriation, that is, all that was his own, may be taken from them. God will judge our righteousness, because "by the deeds of the law there shall no flesh be justified," but by "the righteousness of God, which is by faith" (Rom. iii. 20, 22).

This being understood, I say that, in order that man may be united to his God, wisdom and divine justice, like a pitiless and devouring fire, must take from him all appropriation, all that is terrestrial, carnal, and of his own activity; and having taken all this from him, they must unite him to God.

This is never brought about by the labours of the creature; on the contrary, it even causes him regret, because, as I have said, man so loves what is his own, and is so fearful of its destruction, that if God did not accomplish it Himself, and by His own authority, man would never consent to it.

It will be objected to this, that God never deprives man of his liberty, and that therefore he can always resist God; for which reason I ought not to say that *God acts absolutely, without the consent of man.* In explanation I say, that it is sufficient that man should give a *passive consent*, that he may have entire and full liberty; because having at the beginning given himself to God, that He may do as He will both with him and in him, he gave from that time an *active* and general assent to all that God might do. But when God destroys, burns, and purifies, the soul does not see that all this is for its advantage; it rather believes the contrary: and as at first the fire seems to tarnish the gold, so this operation seems to despoil the soul of its purity. So that if an *active* and *explicit* consent were required, the soul would find a difficulty in giving it, and often would not give it. All that it does is to remain in a passive contentment, enduring this operation as well as it can, being neither able nor willing to prevent it.

God then so purifies this soul of all natural, distinct, and perceived operations, that at last He makes it more and more *conformed* to Himself, and then *uniform*, raising the passive capacity of the creature, enlarging it and ennobling it, though in a hidden and unperceived manner, which is termed mystical. But in all these operations the soul must concur passively, and in proportion as the working of God becomes stronger, the soul must continually yield to Him, until He absorbs it altogether. We do not say, then, as some assert, that there must be no *action*; since, on the contrary, this is *the door*; but only that *we must not remain in it*, seeing that man should tend towards the perfection of his end, and that he can never reach it without quitting the first means, which, though they were necessary to introduce him into the way, would greatly hinder him afterwards, if he attached himself obstinately to them. This is what Paul said, "I forget those things which are behind, and reach forth unto those things which are before; I press toward the mark" (Phil. iii. 13, 14).

Should we not consider a person destitute of reason who, after undertaking a journey, stopped at the first inn, because he was assured that several had passed it, that a few had lodged there, and that the landlord lived there? What the soul is required to do, then, is *to advance towards its end*, to take the shortest road, not to stop at the first point, and, following the advice of St Paul, to suffer itself to be "led by the Spirit of God" (Rom. viii. 14), who will lead it to the end for which it was created, which is the enjoyment of God.

It is well known that the sovereign good is God; that essential blessedness consists in union with God, and that this union cannot be the result of our own efforts, since God only communicates Himself to the soul according to its capacity. We cannot be united to God without passivity and simplicity; and this union being bliss, the way which leads to it must be the best, and there can be no risk in walking in it.

This way is not *dangerous*. If it were, Christ would not have represented it as the most perfect and necessary of all ways. All can walk in it; and as all are called to blessedness, all are called to the enjoyment of God, both in this life and in that which is to come, since the enjoyment of God is blessedness. I say the enjoyment of God Himself, not of His gifts, which can never impart essential blessedness, not being able fully to satisfy the soul, which is so constituted that even the richest gifts of God cannot thoroughly content it. The desire of God is to give Himself to us, according to the capacity with which He has endowed us; and yet we fear to leave ourselves to God! We fear to possess Him, and to be prepared for divine union!

You say, *we must not bring ourselves to this condition.* I agree to that; but I say too, that no one ever could bring himself to it, since no man could ever unite himself to God by his own efforts, and God Himself must do the work.

You say that some pretend to have attained it. I say that this state cannot be feigned, any more than a man dying of hunger can for any length of time pretend to be satisfied. It will soon be known whether or no men have attained this end.

Since, then, none can arrive at the end unless he be brought there, it is not a question of introducing people to it, but of showing them the way which leads to it, and begging them not to rest in those practices which must be relinquished at God's command.

Would it not be cruelty to show a fountain to a thirsty man, and then hold him bound, and prevent his going to it, leaving him to die of thirst? That is what is being done now. Let us all be agreed both as to the way and the end. The way has its commencement, its progress, and its terminus. The more we advance towards the terminus, the farther we go from the commencement; and it is impossible to reach the terminus but by constantly going farther from the starting-point, being unable to go from one place to another without passing through all that comes between them: this is incontestable.

Oh, how blind are the majority of men, who pride themselves upon their learning and talent!

O Lord! how true it is that Thou hast hidden Thy secrets from the wise and prudent, and hast revealed them unto babes